Rewire Your Mind

A 28 Day Spiritual Discovery Journal

Short Reflections to Frame Your Day & Infuse It with Peace

Rewire Your Mind

Short Reflections to Frame Your Day & Infuse It with Peace

MARGARET EATON MADDOX

Blue Violet Press

ISBN-13: 978-0-9967760-7-3

Many thanks to Christina Dreve Young for helping me get this across the finish line.

Thank you to Lisa Huff for designing the cover.

All my love to Robbie for always supporting me, no matter what.

Contents

Why journal?

Journaling can be used for many things: memory keeping, personal growth, therapy, making lists, and reflection. For many people, journaling is fun, valuable, and even life changing.

I have gone through seasons of life where journaling was a regular part of my daily routine. However, journaling has NEVER been something that has come easy. That's why I decided to create this simple journal for you.

Rewire Your Mind is four simple questions to set up your day. If personal inventory isn't something you do on a regular basis, these questions (though simple) may not be easy at first. But with a little practice, journaling can develop a deeper awareness of your inner life.

There are also **Weekly Reviews** so you can pause and look for patterns; **Unraveling Pages**, to dig deeper and reset your day; and a **Word of the Day** list to keep all your words for the month in one place.

Making time to reflect will create a sort of "breathing space" for you, and help you experience a little more peace in your life. (As a Spiritual Director, I believe that the answers to these questions would be great to discuss with your Director!)

I hope you enjoy spending a little time getting to know yourself better.

How to use this book.

Here are some possibilities for using this book (and you can use this book any way that works for you):

- The numbered pages each contain four questions. Schedule time each morning to sit with your journal and answer them. Morning journaling will prepare you for the day, and set the tone and intention for you.

- Find a quiet, comfortable place where you can relax and reflect. Allow whatever comes up for you to be noted in your journal. (But not too comfortable... If you're anything like me, too much comfort makes me sleepy.)

- Keep a special pencil or pen with your journal, one that you look forward to using. Personally I prefer erasable, colored pens. Do everything you can to make this time special, and even fun!

- At the end of seven days, review your answers from the past week. Then go to the weekly reflection for a couple of additional questions.

- This journal also contains some "bonus" journaling material. If you find yourself struggling with anything, take a look at the "Unravel" section.

- At the end of the book, there's an appendix with a "Word of the Day List." It can be enlightening to add your answers from the daily question to this list. You can then see how trends and moods have a natural cycle to them.

Day One.

One thing I would like to accomplish today:_____

_____

_____

_____

One thing I would like to remember today:_____

_____

_____

_____

One thing I love about myself today:_____

_____

_____

_____

My word for today:_____

Day Two.

One thing I would like to accomplish today:_____

_____

_____

_____

One thing I would like to remember today:_____

_____

_____

_____

One thing I love about myself today:_____

_____

_____

_____

My word for today:_____

Day Three.

One thing I would like to accomplish today:_____

_____

_____

_____

One thing I would like to remember today:_____

_____

_____

_____

One thing I love about myself today:_____

_____

_____

_____

My word for today:_____

Day Four.

One thing I would like to accomplish today:_____

_____

_____

_____

One thing I would like to remember today:_____

_____

_____

_____

One thing I love about myself today:_____

_____

_____

_____

My word for today:_____

Day Five.

One thing I would like to accomplish today:_____

_____

_____

_____

One thing I would like to remember today:_____

_____

_____

_____

One thing I love about myself today:_____

_____

_____

_____

My word for today:_____

Day Six.

One thing I would like to accomplish today:_____

_____

_____

_____

One thing I would like to remember today:_____

_____

_____

_____

One thing I love about myself today:_____

_____

_____

_____

My word for today:_____

Day Seven.

One thing I would like to accomplish today:_____

_____

_____

_____

One thing I would like to remember today:_____

_____

_____

_____

One thing I love about myself today:_____

_____

_____

_____

My word for today:_____

Week One.

Take a few moments to review the last seven days of journaling.

What patterns, if any, do you notice in your writing for the last week?

_____

_____

_____

_____

_____

What is a takeaway or learning from the last week?

_____

_____

_____

_____

_____

Day Eight.

One thing I would like to accomplish today:_____

_____

_____

_____

One thing I would like to remember today:_____

_____

_____

_____

One thing I love about myself today:_____

_____

_____

_____

My word for today:_____

Day Nine.

One thing I would like to accomplish today:_____

_____

_____

_____

One thing I would like to remember today:_____

_____

_____

_____

One thing I love about myself today:_____

_____

_____

_____

My word for today:_____

Day Ten.

One thing I would like to accomplish today:_____

_____

_____

_____

One thing I would like to remember today:_____

_____

_____

_____

One thing I love about myself today:_____

_____

_____

_____

My word for today:_____

Day Eleven.

One thing I would like to accomplish today:_____

_____

_____

_____

One thing I would like to remember today:_____

_____

_____

_____

One thing I love about myself today:_____

_____

_____

_____

My word for today:_____

Day Twelve.

One thing I would like to accomplish today:_____

_____

_____

_____

One thing I would like to remember today:_____

_____

_____

_____

One thing I love about myself today:_____

_____

_____

_____

My word for today:_____

Day Thirteen.

One thing I would like to accomplish today:_____

_____

_____

_____

One thing I would like to remember today:_____

_____

_____

_____

One thing I love about myself today:_____

_____

_____

_____

My word for today:_____

Day Fourteen.

One thing I would like to accomplish today:_____

_____

_____

_____

One thing I would like to remember today:_____

_____

_____

_____

One thing I love about myself today:_____

_____

_____

_____

My word for today:_____

Week Two.

Take a few moments to review the last seven days of journaling.

What patterns, if any, do you notice in your writing for the last week?

_____

_____

_____

_____

_____

_____

What is a takeaway or learning from the last week?

_____

_____

_____

_____

Day Fifteen.

One thing I would like to accomplish today:_____

_____

_____

_____

One thing I would like to remember today:_____

_____

_____

_____

One thing I love about myself today:_____

_____

_____

_____

My word for today:_____

Day Sixteen.

One thing I would like to accomplish today:_____

_____

_____

_____

One thing I would like to remember today:_____

_____

_____

_____

One thing I love about myself today:_____

_____

_____

_____

My word for today:_____

Day Seventeen.

One thing I would like to accomplish today:_____

_____

_____

_____

One thing I would like to remember today:_____

_____

_____

_____

One thing I love about myself today:_____

_____

_____

_____

My word for today:_____

Day Eighteen.

One thing I would like to accomplish today:_____

_____

_____

_____

One thing I would like to remember today:_____

_____

_____

_____

One thing I love about myself today:_____

_____

_____

_____

My word for today:_____

Day Nineteen.

One thing I would like to accomplish today:_____

_____

_____

_____

One thing I would like to remember today:_____

_____

_____

_____

One thing I love about myself today:_____

_____

_____

_____

My word for today:_____

Day Twenty.

One thing I would like to accomplish today:_____

_____

_____

_____

One thing I would like to remember today:_____

_____

_____

_____

One thing I love about myself today:_____

_____

_____

_____

My word for today:_____

Day Twenty One.

One thing I would like to accomplish today:_____

_____

_____

_____

One thing I would like to remember today:_____

_____

_____

_____

One thing I love about myself today:_____

_____

_____

_____

My word for today:_____

Week Three.

Take a few moments to review the last seven days of journaling.

What patterns, if any, do you notice in your writing for the last week?

_____

_____

_____

_____

_____

_____

What is a takeaway or learning from the last week?

_____

_____

_____

_____

_____

Day Twenty Two.

One thing I would like to accomplish today:_____

_____

_____

_____

One thing I would like to remember today:_____

_____

_____

_____

One thing I love about myself today:_____

_____

_____

_____

My word for today:_____

Day Twenty Three.

One thing I would like to accomplish today:_____

_____

_____

_____

One thing I would like to remember today:_____

_____

_____

_____

One thing I love about myself today:_____

_____

_____

_____

My word for today:_____

Day Twenty Four.

One thing I would like to accomplish today:_____

_____

_____

_____

One thing I would like to remember today:_____

_____

_____

_____

One thing I love about myself today:_____

_____

_____

_____

My word for today:_____

Day Twenty Five.

One thing I would like to accomplish today:_____

_____

_____

_____

One thing I would like to remember today:_____

_____

_____

_____

One thing I love about myself today:_____

_____

_____

_____

My word for today:_____

Day Twenty Six.

One thing I would like to accomplish today:_____

_____

_____

_____

One thing I would like to remember today:_____

_____

_____

_____

One thing I love about myself today:_____

_____

_____

_____

My word for today:_____

Day Twenty Seven.

One thing I would like to accomplish today:_____

_____

_____

_____

One thing I would like to remember today:_____

_____

_____

_____

One thing I love about myself today:_____

_____

_____

_____

My word for today:_____

Day Twenty Eight.

One thing I would like to accomplish today:_____

_____

_____

_____

One thing I would like to remember today:_____

_____

_____

_____

One thing I love about myself today:_____

_____

_____

_____

My word for today:_____

Week Four.

Take a few moments to review the last seven days of journaling.

What patterns, if any, do you notice in your writing for the last week?

_____

_____

_____

_____

_____

What is a takeaway or learning from the last week?

_____

_____

_____

_____

Unraveling Pages: A Five Minute Mend

These bonus pages are filled with a few questions that you can use to journal when you notice that you are:

- Uneasy
- Uncertain
- Uncomfortable
- Unappreciated
- Undecided
- Unnerved
- Unhappy
- Unsteady
- Unsure

Journaling can help release stress, gain clarity, and/or to learn something about your inner life. Whenever you feel stressed or uncertain, choose one of the five minute mends in this section, set a timer and journal for five minutes. You might be surprised what you learn.

Ready to unravel?

- Find a quiet place.

- Center yourself by taking three deep breaths and grounding your body.

- Choose a question that appeals to you.

- Set a timer for 5 minutes and write without censoring yourself.

Mind Mend One:

- What do I need right now?
- What would it look like to ask for what I need?
- Who do I need to ask: someone else? Myself? God?

_____

_____

_____

_____

_____

_____

_____

Mind Mend Two:

- Is there anything that I should be doing or carrying myself, that I'm asking someone else to handle? Is there something I should be taking responsibility for instead of delegating?
- What would it be like to remove that burden from them and carry it for myself?

Mind Mend Three:

- If I could change one thing about my life right now, what would it be?
- Why would I change it? What steps could I take to move forward with that change?

_____

_____

_____

_____

_____

_____

_____

Mind Mend Four:

• My biggest fear right now is...(fill in the blank). What would it be
  like to face this fear?

_____

_____

_____

_____

_____

_____

_____

_____

Mind Mend Five:

• Is there anything that I am currently doing or carrying that belongs to someone else? What would it be like to release that burden?

_____

_____

_____

_____

_____

_____

_____

Mind Mend Six:

• What am I struggling with right now?

• If I were to stop resisting, what positives might result for me?

• What is the invitation for me in this struggle?

Mind Mend Seven:

• Take an inventory of your physical body.
• Ask: What do I feel right now? What is my body trying to tell me?

_____

_____

_____

_____

_____

_____

_____

Mind Mend Eight:

- What help do I need?
- Are there any unexpected places from which help could come? Ask God for openness to see a new way.

_____

_____

_____

_____

_____

_____

_____

Word of the Day List

Day 1 _____

Day 2 _____

Day 3 _____

Day 4 _____

Day 5 _____

Day 6 _____

Day 7 _____

Day 8 _____

Day 9 _____

Day 10 _____

Day 11 _____

Day 12 _____

Day 13 _____

Day 14 _____

Day 15 _____

Day 16 _____

Day 17 _____

Day 18 _____

Day 19 _____

Day 20 _____

Day 21 _____

Day 22 _____

Day 23 _____

Day 24 _____

Day 25 _____

Day 26 _____

Day 27 _____

Day 28 _____

ABOUT THE AUTHOR

Margaret is a spiritual director who helps people get still and hear
their "still, small voice." She has helped clients find peace
during times of challenge, achieve clarity for important life decisions,
and discover ways to more personally connect with God.
Margaret lives in northern Kentucky with her husband
and their two dogs, Rocky Romeo and Shadeaux Luna.
When they are living their best life, you can find
the four of them camping and hiking across the U.S.

If you would like to connect with Margaret, you can find her at
margaretmaddox.com

CPSIA information can be obtained
at www.ICGtesting.com
Printed in the USA
LVHW100258100919
630430LV00011B/1004/P